Looking at Science
How Things Change

Looking at
WEATHER
AND SEASONS

HOW DO THEY CHANGE?

Angela Royston

Enslow Elementary
an imprint of
Enslow Publishers, Inc.
40 Industrial Road
Box 398
Berkeley Heights, NJ 07922
USA
http://www.enslow.com

Enslow Elementary, an imprint of Enslow Publishers, Inc.

Enslow Elementary® is a registered trademark of Enslow Publishers, Inc.

This edition published in 2008 by Enslow Publishers, Inc.

Library of Congress Cataloging-in-Publication Data

Royston, Angela.
  Looking at weather and seasons : how do they change? / Angela Royston.
    p. cm. — (Looking at science : how things change)
  Summary: "An introductory look at what causes Earth's weather and seasons"—
Provided by publisher.
  Includes bibliographical references and index.
  ISBN-13: 978-0-7660-3093-0 (alk. paper)
  ISBN-10: 0-7660-3093-8 (alk. paper)
1. Weather—Juvenile literature. 2. Seasons—Juvenile literature. I. Title.
  QC981.3.R68 2008
  551.6—dc22

                          2007024515

Printed in the United States of America

10 9 8 7 6 5 4 3 2 1

To Our Readers: We have done our best to make sure all Internet Addresses in this book were active and appropriate when we went to press. However, the author and the publisher have no control over and assume no liability for the material available on those Internet sites or on other Web sites they may link to. Any comments or suggestions can be sent by e-mail to comments@enslow.com or to the address on the back cover.

Every effort has been made to locate all copyright holders of material used in this book. If any errors or omissions have occurred, corrections will be made in future editions of this book.

For The Brown Reference Group plc
Project Editor: Sarah Eason
Designer: Paul Myerscough
Picture Researcher: Maria Joannou
Children's Publisher: Anne O'Daly

Photo and Illustration Credits: Alamy Images/SuperStock, p. 8B; Bananastock, pp. 4, 16; Corbis/Mark Gamba, p. 12; Dreamstime, pp. 1, 5T, 17; istockphoto, pp. 2, 8, 10, 10B, 12B, 14, 19T, 19B, 20, 22, 24B, 25B, 28, 29T; Photos.com, 6B, 7B, 18, 23, 26, 26B; Science Photo Library, p. 10T; Shutterstock, pp. 6, 11B, 13B, 20B, 21C, 23T, 24, 27T, 28B, 30; Geoff Ward (illustrations), pp. 7, 14, 15.
Cover Photo: Dreamstime

Contents

What is weather?

The weather can change from day to day. It can be hot or cold. It can be sunny, cloudy, rainy, or windy. Sometimes it even snows.

In a thunderstorm, flashes of lightning are followed by thunder. It may rain too.

People like to be ▶ outside when the weather is nice.

4

▲ Sometimes the weather is stormy.
Then it is safest to stay inside!

People choose different clothes
for different kinds of weather.
When it is hot, they might wear
shorts. When it is cold, they might
wear coats, hats, and mittens.

What makes the weather warm?

The Sun is very far away, but it is very hot. Heat from the Sun reaches the Earth and makes the Earth warm.

The Sun rises in the morning and sets in the evening. At noon the Sun is almost overhead in the sky. This is when the Sun is highest in the sky.

It is noon in this picture. The Sun is overhead in the sky.

6

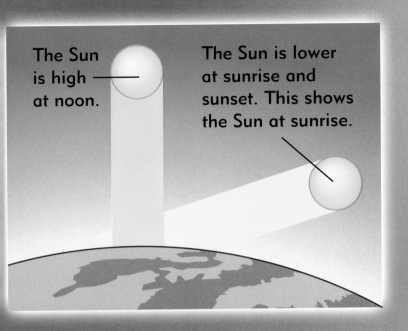

The Sun is high at noon.

The Sun is lower at sunrise and sunset. This shows the Sun at sunrise.

◄ The Sun's rays are strongest when the Sun is high in the sky. They are weakest when the Sun is close to the horizon at sunrise and sunset.

The Sun's rays are very strong. You should never look directly at the Sun.

The Sun is setting ► in this picture. The day will soon change to night.

Where does rain come from?

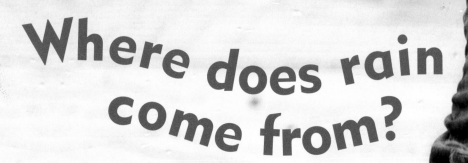

Clouds are made of tiny droplets of water. The droplets join to make raindrops.

As the raindrops become bigger, they become heavier. When the raindrops are too heavy to stay in the cloud, they fall as rain.

◄ An umbrella, a raincoat, and boots help keep you dry.

The ground soaks up rain. Rain also runs into streams, lakes, and rivers.

Puddles form on the ground where the rain cannot be soaked up, such as on roads. Puddles dry up when the Sun comes out and warms them.

◄ When it rains a lot, some of the rain forms puddles on the ground.

What are snow and hail?

When the air is very cold, the water droplets in a cloud freeze to make snow instead of rain. Sometimes raindrops freeze in the cloud to make hail.

◀ Hail is harder and bigger than snowflakes.

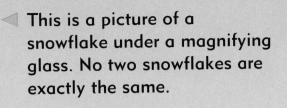

◄ This is a picture of a snowflake under a magnifying glass. No two snowflakes are exactly the same.

If the ground is warm, snow and hail melt soon. If it is cold, snow can stay on the ground for days, weeks, or even months. Sometimes the snow can become very deep.

Snow can be fun to ► play in if you are warmly dressed.

What is wind?

Wind is moving air. When it is windy you can feel the air blowing in your face. The wind shakes the leaves and bends the branches of trees.

The wind lifts a ▷ kite into the air.

The faster air moves, the stronger the wind is. A breeze is a very light wind. The strongest winds are made by hurricanes and tornadoes. Everyone must find shelter during a hurricane or tornado.

▲ The wind in a hurricane or tornado is so strong it can blow over trees and damage some buildings.

What will the weather be like?

Clouds can sometimes show us what the weather will be like. If a cloud is dark gray or black, it may be heavy with raindrops. This means that it may soon rain.

▼ Different kinds of clouds have different names. Cumulus and stratus clouds can both bring rain.

Cumulus clouds are puffy.

Stratus clouds are low and spread out.

Cirrus clouds are high and wispy.

Weather satellites travel ▷ around the Earth high above the clouds. They take photographs of the clouds.

A weather satellite sends a picture to Earth.

Meteorologists are scientists who study the weather. They use special tools to measure weather.

Computers and weather satellites help meteorologists figure out how the weather might change.

What are the seasons?

The weather changes from day to day, but it also changes during the year. Some months of the year are hotter than other months. These changes are called the seasons.

◀ These children are dressed for warm summer weather.

There are four seasons—winter, spring, summer, and fall.
Winter is the coldest season and summer is the warmest season.

These children are dressed for cold winter weather.

What happens in winter?

Winter is the coldest time of the year. In many places it snows. The water in ponds and lakes may turn to ice.

In winter, the nights are longer and the days are shorter. It is too cold for most plants to grow.

▲ Many trees have no leaves in winter.

Many animals, such as this squirrel, store food for the winter.

Some animals make a den or a burrow and stay in it all winter. This is called hibernation.

A black bear hibernates during winter.

What happens in spring?

During spring the weather gets warmer. The days grow longer and the nights become shorter. New leaves grow on the trees, and plants and flowers grow.

▼ In spring, the buds on trees begin to open into new leaves and flowers.

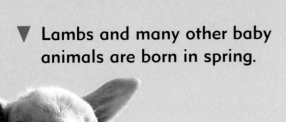

▼ Lambs and many other baby animals are born in spring.

Birds build nests and lay eggs. Many animals give birth to their young. The warmer weather makes it easier for baby animals to survive.

This bird has made ▲ a nest. It will lay its eggs inside the nest.

What happens in summer?

Summer is the warmest season. The days are long and the nights are short.

Young animals grow bigger in summer. The hot sunshine makes fruits grow bigger, too. They slowly become ripe and ready to eat. Crops, such as wheat and corn, become ripe.

◀ Green tomatoes change to red as they grow ripe.

▲ Corn grows very
tall in summer!

People spend ▶
more time
outside
in summer.

What happens in fall?

In fall, the days become shorter and the nights become longer. The weather becomes cooler, too. Animals get ready for winter. The leaves on some trees change color and fall to the ground.

◀ These leaves have changed color from green to red, yellow, and brown.

Many animals eat extra food in fall. They become fatter, which helps them to stay alive in winter when there is little food. After winter spring comes, and the seasons begin all over again.

Chipmunks bury nuts in fall to last throughout the winter.

How do we use the weather?

We use weather to help us grow food, make energy, and have fun! Rain brings water for plants and crops. The Sun makes plants and crops grow.

▼ All plants need sunlight to grow bigger.

At the beach, people use ▷
wind to windsurf in the
water, or to fly kites.
And lots of people like
to play in the sunshine!

Wind makes
wind turbines
turn around,
which makes
energy. The
heat from
the Sun can
be used to keep houses
and buildings warm.

▲ On a windy day, these
wind turbines spin around
very quickly. That makes
a lot of energy!

27

What do I know about weather?

1. Keep a weather diary for a week. Look outside every day and write down:
   - If it is sunny, rainy, cold, or warm.
   - How the weather changes during the day.
   - How many days were dry.
   - How many days were wet.
   - Which day was the hottest and which day was the coldest.

2. Think about the weather when you choose your clothes. Are the clothes you have chosen right for the weather?

3. Try flying a kite when the weather is windy. What happens when the wind blows strongly?

4. Write down how the ground changes when it is rainy and when it is dry. What happens?

Words to Know

burrow — A hole in the ground in which animals live.

den — An animal's shelter or hiding place.

hail — Raindrops that freeze in a cloud and fall as ice.

hibernation — When animals stay inside a den or burrow during winter to keep warm.

horizon — Where the sky appears to meet the ground.

hurricane — A strong storm with very powerful winds that can cause a lot of damage.

lightning — Flashes of electricity in the sky during a thunderstorm.

magnifying glass — An instrument that makes things look larger than they really are.

meteorologist — A scientist who studies the weather.

thunderstorm — A storm that includes thunder and lightning.

tornado — A dangerous storm that has a tight circle of very strong wind.

weather satellite — A machine that studies Earth's weather from space.

Learn More

Books

Cosgrove, Brian. *Weather*. New York: DK Publishing (2004).

Eckart, Edana. *Watching the Weather: Watching Nature*. New York: Children's Press (2004).

Macaulay, Kelley and Bobbie Kalman. *Changing Weather: Storms*. New York: Crabtree Publishing Company (2006).

Web Sites

Snow Crystals

www.snowcrystals.com

The Weather Dude

www.wxdude.com

Weather Wiz Kids

www.weatherwizkids.com

Index